VETERINARIANS

by Golriz Golkar

cone

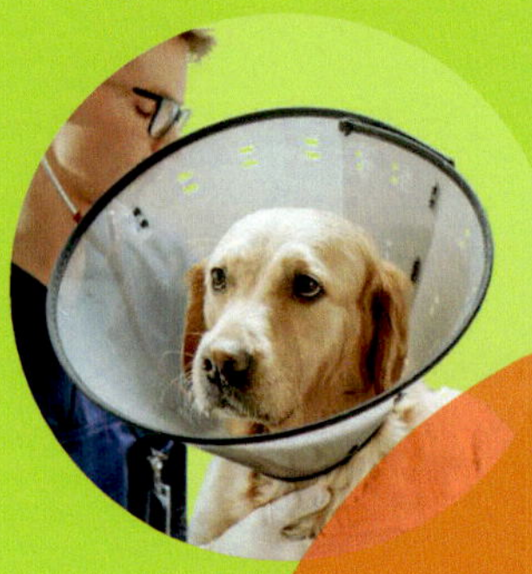

shot

Look for these words and pictures as you read.

hamster

bandage

Veterinarians help us.
What do they do?

The office is busy.
Many pets wait for the vet.

cone
The dog has a cut.
He wears a cone.
It stops him from
scratching his cut.

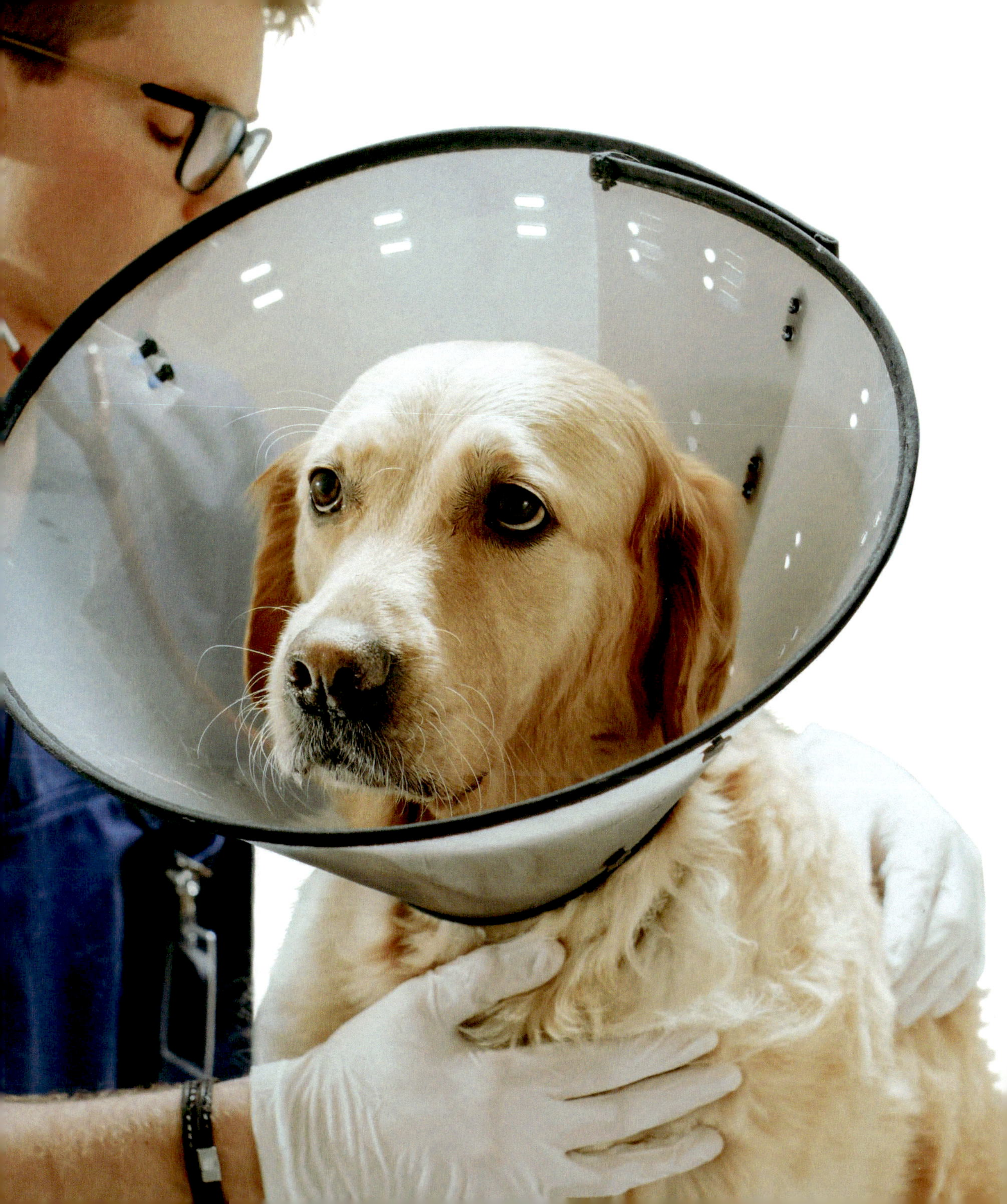

This cat gets a shot.
It keeps the cat healthy.
Meow!
shot

hamster

Uh-oh!

This hamster is sick.

The vet checks its heart.

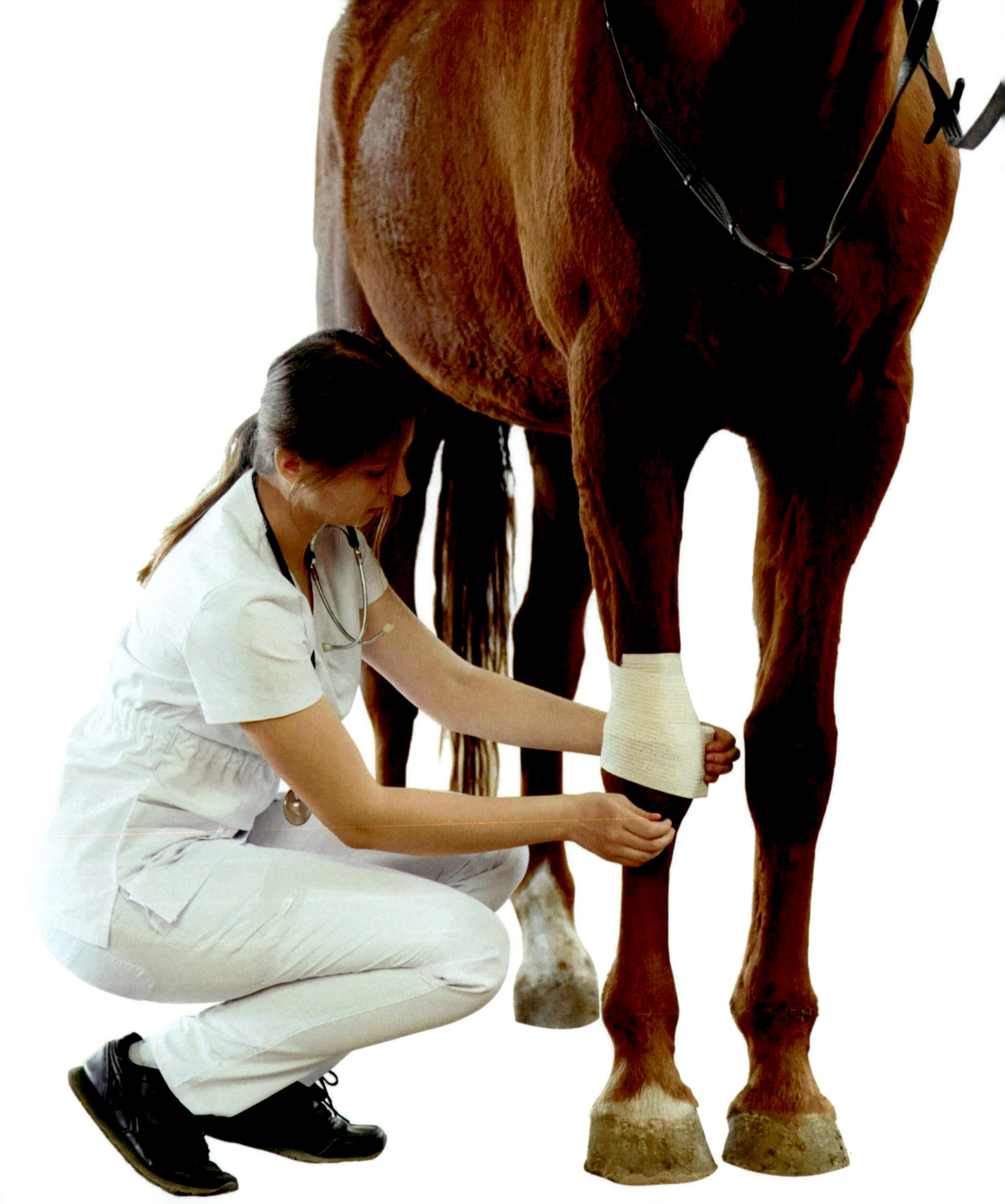

bandage

This horse has a hurt leg.

It gets a bandage.

Much better!

Vets are animal doctors.
They make animals feel better.

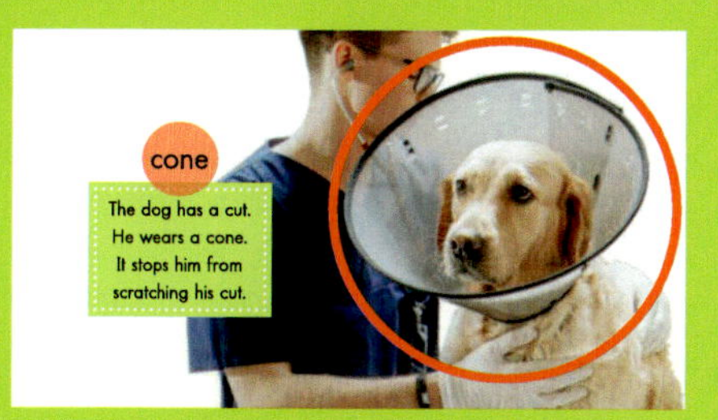

cone

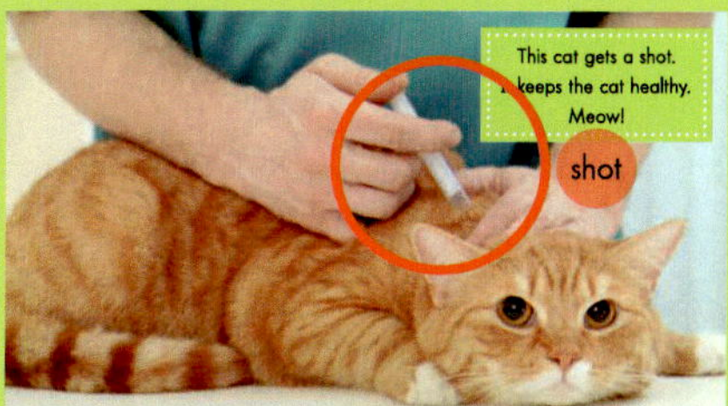

shot

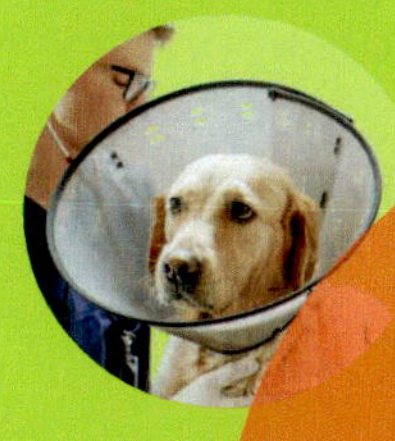

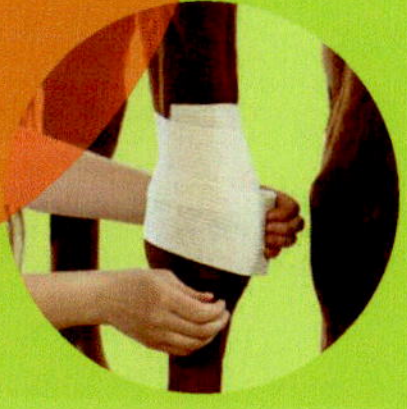

Did you find?

hamster

bandage

Spot is published by Amicus Learning, an imprint of Amicus
P.O. Box 227, Mankato, MN 56002
www.amicuspublishing.us

Library of Congress Cataloging-in-Publication Data
Names: Golkar, Golriz, author.
Title: Veterinarians / by Golriz Golkar.
Description: Mankato, MN : Amicus Learning, [2026] |
    Series: Spot community helpers | Audience: Ages 4–7 |
    Audience: Grades K–1 | Summary: "Veterinarians are
    doctors for animals. They keep our pets healthy! Learn
    how they help the community in this low-level beginning
    reader that reinforces new vocabulary with a search-
    and-find feature. A great early social studies book that
    will inspire kindergartners and first graders to learn
    about jobs in their community"– Provided by publisher.
Identifiers: LCCN 2024043691 (print) | LCCN 2024043692
    (ebook) | ISBN 9798892004947 (library binding) |
    ISBN 9798892005487 (paperback) |
    ISBN 9798892006026 (ebook)
Subjects: LCSH: Veterinarians—Juvenile literature. |
    Veterinary medicine—Juvenile literature.
Classification: LCC SF756 .G65 2026 (print) | LCC SF756
    (ebook) | DDC 636.089092–dc23/eng/20250102
LC record available at https://lccn.loc.gov/2024043691
LC ebook record available at https://lccn.loc.
    gov/2024043692

Ana Brauer, editor
Deb Miner, series designer
Sara Hood, book designer
 and photo researcher

Photos by Getty Images/AzmanL,
4–5, elenaleonova, 8–9, Fuse, 3;
Shutterstock/aslysun, cover, Beach
Creatives, 14, DnDavis, 1, Gorodenkoff,
6–7, santypan, 10–11, Standret, 12

VETERINARIANS